AF426384

action	comportamiento	Action!
actually	Realmente	I actually like strawberry.
adjective	adjetivo	Tell me an adjective to describe this.
afraid	asustado	What are you afraid of?
agreed	convenido	They agreed on music.
ahead	adelante	Who was ahead in the race?
allow	permitir	Did the teacher allow him to play?
apple	manzana	Eat an apple.
arrived	llegado	My plane arrived on time.
born	nacido	Where were you born?
bought	compró	She bought new clothes.
British	británico	Who is the British monarch?
capital	capital	The capital is in Washington, DC.
chance	oportunidad	Dice is a game of chance.
chart	gráfico	What does your medical chart say?
church	Iglesia	Did you go to church?
column	columna	Did you read the newspaper column?
company	empresa	What company do you work for?
conditions	condiciones	What are the weather conditions.
corn	maíz	Do you like corn?
cotton	algodón	A q-tip is made of cotton.
cows	vaca	How many cows does he have?
create	crear	What art did you create?
dead	muerto	The bug is dead.

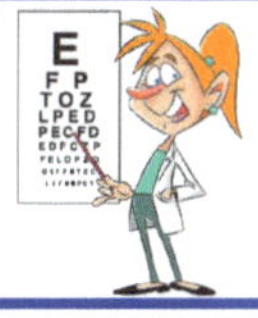

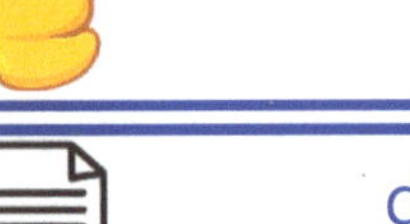

deal — acuerdo

Did you agree on the deal?

death — muerte

The grim reaper is death.

details — detalles

Look for the details.

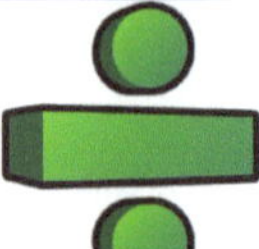

determine — determinar

Did you determine where to eat?

difficult — difícil

I found this difficult.

division — división

We learned division today.

doesn't — no

Doesn't it sound beautiful?

effect — efecto

How did the medicine effect your cold?

entire — todo

The entire family was in the picture.

especially — especialmente

She especially liked writing.

evening — noche

The ceremony was this evening.

experience — experiencia

She has a lot of experience.

factories — suerte

There are a lot of factories there.

fair — parque alegre

Let's go to the fair.

fear — miedo

I have a huge fear of clowns.

fig — higos

I ate a fig.

forward — adelante

Spring forward the clocks.

France — Francia

Have you ever been to France?

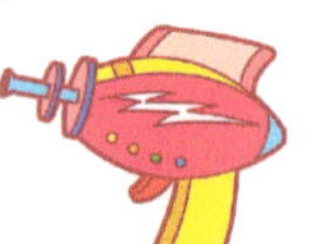

fresh — Fresco

All the fruit is fresh.

Greek — griego

Have you ever had Greek food?

gun — pistola

We played with a water gun.

hoe — azada

Use a hoe in the garden.

huge — enorme

Those trees are huge!

isn't — no es

Isn't it nice to hang out with friends?

 led — líder
The dog led her.

 level — nivel
Use the level to hang the picture.

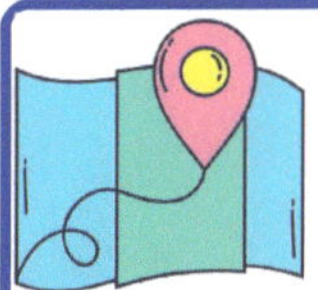 located — situado
Where is the store located?

 march — desfile
Are you going to march with the band?

 match — partido
Did you match them?

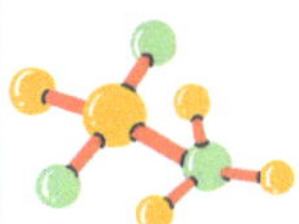 molecules — moléculas
Are those molecules?

 northern — del Norte
He lives in northern California.

 nose — nariz
My nose is running.

 office — oficina
Do you need any office supplies?

 oxygen — oxígeno
What is the symbol for oxygen?

 plural — plural
What is the plural of a mouse?

 prepared — preparar
She prepared for the exam.

 pretty — bonita
Pretty in pink.

 printed — impreso
She printed out the forms.

 radio — radio
Let's listen to the radio.

 repeated — repetir
They repeated the exercises daily.

 rope — cuerda
Do you have any rope?

 rose — Rosa
Thank you for the rose.

 score — Puntuación
What was the final score?

 seat — asiento
The girls took a seat in the sand.

 settled — colocado
The case was settled.

 shoes — Zapatos
Put your shoes on.

 shop — tienda
I'm need to go shop for groceries.

 similar — similar
The halves are similar.

sir — *señor*
Yes, sir!

sister — *hermana*
Is she your sister?

smell — *oler*
I love the smell of cookies!

solution — *solución*
I figured out a solution!

southern — *meridional*
She's a southern belle.

steel — *acero*
The new building used steel.

stretched — *estirado*
We stretched before the workout.

substances — *sustancias*
What are these substances?

suffix — *sufijo*
What is the suffix of the word?

sugar — *azúcar*
Sugar cube for your tea?

tools — *herramientas*
May I borrow your tools?

total — *total*
What's the total?

track — *pista*
The runners got on the track.

triangle — *triángulo*
How many sides does a triangle have?

truck — *camión*
Is thaty our truck?

underline — *subrayar*

Underline the word.

various — *varios*
I watch various shows.

view — *ver*
That is a beautiful view!

Washington — *Washington*
She is from Washington.

we'll — *será*
We'll finish buying our groceries.

western — *occidental*
It's western wear day.

win — *ganar*
Did you win?

woman — *mujer*
The woman was on her way to work.

workers — *trabajadores*
The workers were busy.

wouldn't — no

Wouldn't you like to go shopping?

yellow — amarillo

A banana is yellow.

again — de nuevo

May we go on the ride again?

also — además

I also like baseball.

animal — animal

My favorite animal is a lion.

answer — responder

Raise your hand to answer.

around — alrededor

Let's travel around the world.

away — lejos

Throw your trash away.

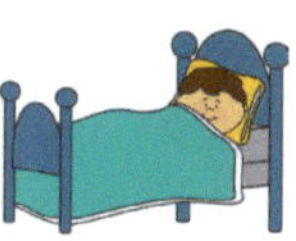

because — porque

I went to bed because I was tired.

big — grande

The elephant is a big animal.

came — vino

He came to class.

different — diferente

They use different balls.

wrong — incorrecto

Did I get it wrong?

after — después

You may have dessert after dinner.

air — aire

The air was cold.

America — America

Columbus sailed to America.

another — otro

Have another cookie.

any — ninguna

Do you have any crayons?

ask — pedir

It's good to ask questions.

back — espalda

We went back to school.

before — antes de

Sharpen your pencil before the test.

boy — chico

The boy played a basketball.

change — cambio

I save my change.

does — hacer

Does he ride the bus?

end — *final*
She watched to the end.

even — *incluso*
They learned about even numbers.

follow — *seguir*
Follow the teacher.

form — *formar*
Complete the form.

found — *encontró*
We found a puppy.

give — *dar*
I like to give gifts.

good — *bueno*
The hamburger was good.

great — *estupendo*
Great job!

hand — *mano*
Please hand in your work.

help — *ayuda*
You should help others.

here — *aquí*
Do you sit here?

home — *casa*
Is this your home?

house — *casa*
The doll house was pink.

just — *sólo*
The train just left.

kind — *se amable*
Be kind to each other.

know — *saber*
I don't know.

land — *tierra*
They bought some land.

large — *grande*
A bear is large.

learn — *aprender*
It's fun to learn science.

letter — *carta*
He mailed a letter.

line — *líneas*
Please form a line.

little — *pequeño*
He has a little sister.

live — *En Vivo*
You live in the city.

man — *hombre*
The man drove.

me	yo	Come with me to the park.
men	hombres	The men played football.
mother	madre	He loves his mother.
much	mucho	How much is the camera?
name	nombre	What is his name?
new	nuevo	We have a new teacher.
old	antiguo	Those are old toys.
our	nuestra	She was our teacher.
page	página	Please turn the page.
place	sitio	This is my favorite place.
point	punto	Point the way.
read	leer	Do you like to read?
means	medio	She got her by means of a taxi.
most	más	Most students like to help.
move	moverse	His family decided to move.
must	debe	You must raise your hand.
need	querer	Do you need to sleep?
off	apagado	The rocket blasted off.
only	solamente	There's only one slice left.
over	terminado	He jumped over it.
picture	imagen	They took their picture.
play	jugar	Let's play together!
put	poner	Please put the supplies away.
right	Correcto	That's a right triangle.

same — mismo

Did you get the same answer?

say — decir

What did you say?

sentence — frase

Complete the sentence.

set — conjunto

Please set the table.

should — debería

We should exercise.

show — show

Show your work.

small — pequeña

The ladybug is small.

sound — sonido

A bee makes a buzzing sound.

spell — deletrear

Please spell the word.

still — todavía

I still want ice skates.

study — estudiar

It's time to study.

such — tal

He is such a good dog.

take — tomar

Please take your seat.

tell — contar

She wanted to tell a secret.

things — cosas

She washed a lot of things.

think — pensar

Think about it.

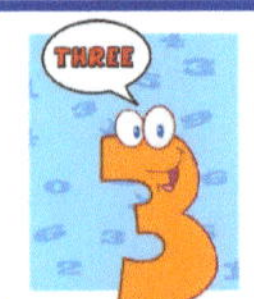
three — Tres

It's the number three.

through — mediante

He was through with the race.

too — también

Do you like chocolate too?

try — tratar

Try again, please.

turn — giro

Turn in your homework.

us — nosotros

She taught us.

very — muy

He is a very good singer.

want — querer

I want to ride my bike.

 **well** — bien
You did well.

 **went** — se fue
We went to recess.

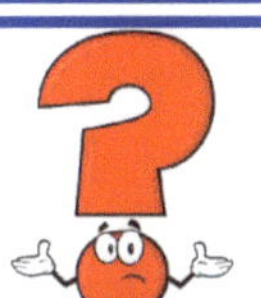 **where** — dónde
Where do you want to go?

 **why** — por qué
She asked why?

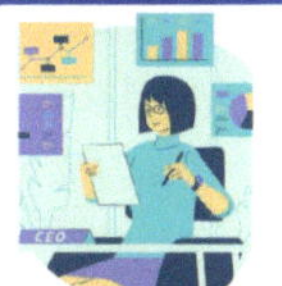 **work** — trabajo
Hard work pays off.

 **world** — mundo
I want to travel the world.

 **years** — años
You are five years old today.

 **above** — encima
The sky was above them.

 **add** — añadir
If you add one plus two, you get three.

 **almost** — casi
It's almost lunch time.

 **along** — a lo largo
We get along.

 **always** — siempre
She always brushes her teeth.

 **began** — empezó
The baby began to cry.

 **begin** — empezar
You may begin your exam.

 **being** — siendo
She is being shy.

 **below** — abajo
It's below thirty degrees.

 **between** — Entre
Two is between one and three.

 **book** — libro
I'm reading this book.

 **both** — ambos
They both worked on math.

 **car** — coche
He bought a new car.

 **carry** — llevar
She had a bag to carry her groceries.

 **children** — niños
Four children sang.

 **city** — ciudad
He worked in the city.

 **close** — cerca
Please close the door.

 **country** — país
Do you live in the country?

 **cut** — cortar
You use scissors to cut.

 **don't** — no
Don't forget!

 **earth** — tierra
Our planet is Earth.

 **eat** — comer
I eat bananas.

 **enough** — suficiente
Did you eat enough pancakes?

 **every** — cada
I shower every day.

 **example** — ejemplo
This is an example of a bird.

 **eyes** — ojos
What color are her eyes?

 **face** — cara
They were at the face painting booth.

 **family** — familia
How big is your family?

 **far** — lejos
How far is it?

 **father** — padre
Her father walked her to school.

 **feet** — pies
Put socks on your feet.

 **few** — pocos
She wanted a few more minutes.

 **food** — comida
They made a lot of food.

 **four** — cuatro
There were four of them.

 **girl** — niña
The girl wore pink shoes.

 **got** — tiene
She got a hair cut.

 **group** — grupo
They were working in a group.

 **grow** — crecer
The plant began to grow.

 **hard** — difícil
He wore a hard hat.

 **head** — cabeza
He wore a cap on his head.

 **hear** — oír
You hear through your ears.

high — *alto*

She wore high heels.

idea — *idea*

I have an idea!

important — *importante*

It's important!

Indian — *indio*

It's an Indian elephant.

it's — *es*

It's a tiger cub.

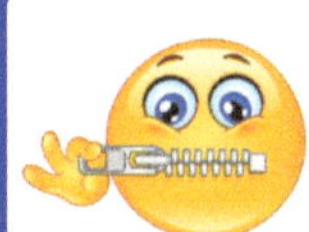

keep — *mantener*

Can you keep a secret?

last — *último*

It's the last day of school.

late — *tarde*

You're late.

leave — *salir*

He packed to leave.

left — *izquierda*

Are you left or right handed?

let — *dejar*

Will you let me go fishing?

life — *vida*

Life is about friends and family.

light — *la luz*

The light turned yellow.

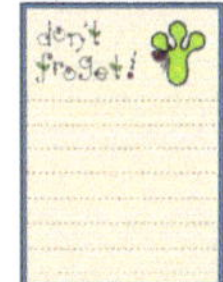

list — *lista*

Here's my to-do list

might — *podría*

It might rain today.

mile — *milla*

It's a mile from here.

miss — *pierda*

You may correct any you miss.

mountains — *montaña*

There are alot of mountains here.

near — *cerca*

We are near the beach.

never — *Nunca*

I've never broken my leg.

next — *siguiente*

Take the next step.

night — *noche*

You can see the stars at night.

often — *a menudo*

How often do you watch tv?

once — *una vez*

Once upon a time...

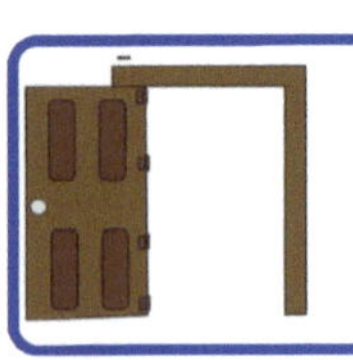
open — abierto
The door is open.

own — propio
Do you own a computer?

paper — papel
Do you have paper towels?

plant — planta
I will water the plant.

real — real
Her real name is Sally.

river — río
The river is high.

run — correr
He likes to run with his dog.

saw — ver
We saw a UFO.

school — colegio
Do you like school?

sea — mar
The ship is at sea.

second — segundo
She won second place.

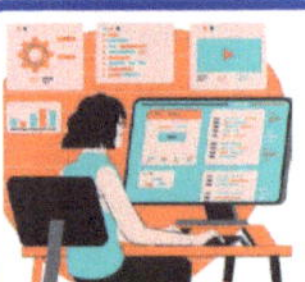
seem — parecer
You seem busy.

side — lado
Each side of a square is the same.

something — alguna cosa
Did you hear something?

sometimes — algunas veces
Sometimes we watch tv.

song — canción
We will sing a song.

soon — pronto
Dinner will be ready soon.

start — comienzo
Start writing.

state — estado
Which state do you live in?

stop — detener
Do you see the stop sign?

story — historia
What's the story about?

talk — hablar
Let's talk.

those — aquellos
Those are great cookies!

thought — pensamiento
I thought the novel was good.

together — juntos

They went shopping together.

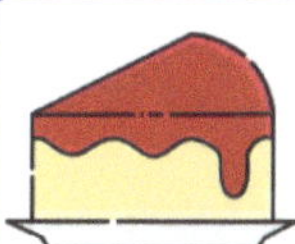

took — tomar

He took the last piece.

tree — árbol

Did you decorate the tree?

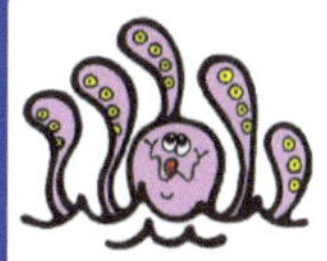

under — debajo

It lives under the sea.

until — hasta

I work until 5 o'clock.

walk — caminar

We went for a walk.

watch — reloj de pulsera

Do you wear a watch?

while — mientras

We had fun while skiing.

white — blanco

They drew on the white board.

without — sin

I can't go without my backpack.

young — joven

Her kids are young.

across — a través de

It's across the street.

against — en contra

It's against the rules.

area — zona

There are no wild animals in this area.

become — volverse

It will become a butterfly.

best — mejor

Do your best!

better — mejor

Feel better soon!

birds — pájaro

There's a lot of birds.

black — negro

He has a black cat.

body — cuerpo

The body has a lot of bones.

certain — cierto

Certain words are harder than others.

cold — frío

It's cold outside.

color — color

What is your favorite color?

complete — completar

Did you complete your workout?

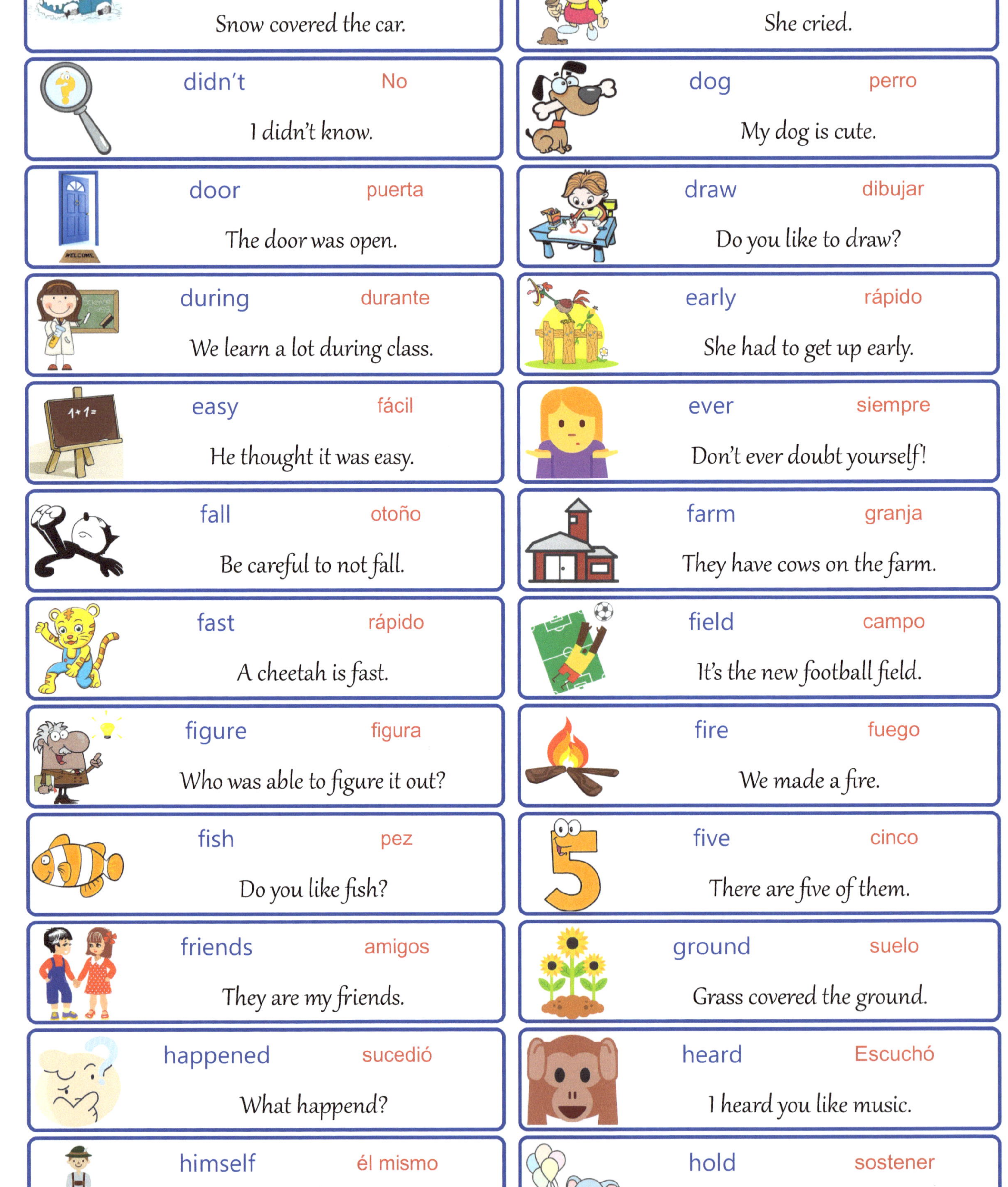

covered — cubrir
Snow covered the car.
cried — llorar
She cried.
didn't — No
I didn't know.
dog — perro
My dog is cute.
door — puerta
The door was open.
draw — dibujar
Do you like to draw?
during — durante
We learn a lot during class.
early — rápido
She had to get up early.
easy — fácil
He thought it was easy.
ever — siempre
Don't ever doubt yourself!
fall — otoño
Be careful to not fall.
farm — granja
They have cows on the farm.
fast — rápido
A cheetah is fast.
field — campo
It's the new football field.
figure — figura
Who was able to figure it out?
fire — fuego
We made a fire.
fish — pez
Do you like fish?
five — cinco
There are five of them.
friends — amigos
They are my friends.
ground — suelo
Grass covered the ground.
happened — sucedió
What happend?
heard — Escuchó
I heard you like music.
himself — él mismo
He smiled to himself.
hold — sostener
Hold on to the balloons!

horse — caballo

Have you ever riden a horse?

hours — horas

How many hours is it open?

however — sin embargo

He hates milk, however he drank it.

hundred — cien

She made a one hundred on the quiz.

I'll — será

I'll call.

king — Rey

Have you ever met a king?

knew — sabia

She knew the doctor.

listen — escucha

Do you listen to music?

low — bajo

My battery is low.

map — mapa

Did you look at the map?

mark — marca

I used a check mark.

measure — medida

Did you measure it?

money — dinero

How much money have you saved?

morning — Mañana

Do you drink coffee in the morning?

music — música

I love music.

north — norte

Go north.

notice — aviso

Put the notice on the board.

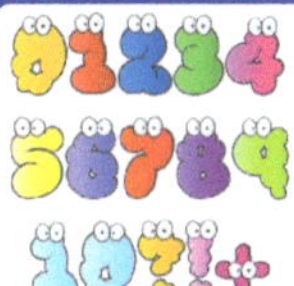

numeral — número

Which numeral did you choose?

order — secuencia

Put them in order of date.

passed — pasado

She passed her driver's exam.

pattern — modelo

Which dress pattern?

piece — pedazo

This piece fits.

plan — plan

Look at the house plan.

problem — problema

Let's solve the problem.

products — productos

Which products do you like?

pulled — tirado

He pulled the wagon.

questions — preguntas

Do you have questions?

reached — alcanzado

You reached high for your goals.

red — rojo

It's a red heart.

remember — recuerda

I'll try to remember.

rock — rock

A diamond is part of a rock.

room — habitación

They hang out in this room.

seen — visto

Have any of you seen the movie?

several — varios

They looked at several creatures.

ship — Embarcacion

The ship sailed.

short — corto

You cut your hair short.

since — ya que

Since you like cookies, let's make some.

sing — canta

We sing.

slowly — despacio

The turtle walked slowly.

south — sur

Mexico is south of the US.

space — cosmos

The astronaut went to space.

stand — estar

Please stand up.

step — paso

Here's the step ladder.

sun — Dom

The sun was out.

sure — Por supuesto

Sure, I'll go to the magic show!

table — mesa

Please sit at the table.

today — hoy

Today we'll go to the pool.

told — dicho

I told you I made a snowman.

top — parte superior

We put a cherry on top.

toward — hacia

She taught toward the front.

town — pueblo

Meet at the town square.

travel — viajar

Let's travel.

TRUE — cierto

It's true love.

unit — unidad

A centimeter is a unit of length.

upon — sobre

Once upon a time there was a princess.

usually — generalmente

Usually I have coffee.

voice — voz

Use your quiet voice.

vowel — vocal

What are vowels?

war — guerra

The war of the Empire and the Republic.

waves — olas

The waves were great for surfing.

whole — todo

Were you sick the whole time?

wind — viento

The wind is too strong.

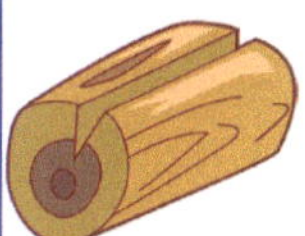
wood — madera

Did you chop the wood?

able — poder

Are you able to ride a bike?

ago — hace

It happened a long time ago.

am — es

I am hungry.

among — entre

He was among the chairs.

ball — pelota

He was among the chairs.

base — béisbol

Do you play first base?

became — convirtió

She became a nurse.

behind — detrás

The cow was behind the fence.

boat — barco

Did you want to go on the boat?

box — caja

What's in the box?

bring — traer

Bring your friends!

brought — trajo

Everyone brought a present.

building — edificio

I made a building with legos.

built — construido

He built a house.

cannot — no puedo

You cannot succeed without hard work.

carefully — Cuidado

Handle those carefully.

check — cheque

Did you get a check mark?

circle — circulo

She drew a circle.

class — clase

It's a class party.

clear — claro

The glass is clear.

common — común

They have a lot in common.

contain — Contiene

What stories does it contain?

correct — correcto

Was that the correct piece?

course — curso

Did you go to the golf course?

dark — oscuro

It's dark at night.

decided — decidir

We decided to go to the lake.

deep — profundo

The ocean is very deep.

done — hecho

Well done!

dry — seco

Try to stay dry.

English — Inglés

Do you enjoy English class?

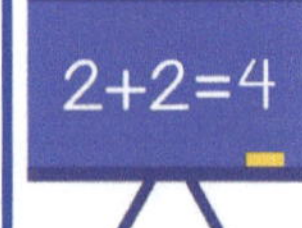

equation — ecuación

Find the answer to the equation.

explain — explique

Please explain it again.

fact — hecho

Is that a fact or opinion?

| feel | sensación |

How do you feel?

| filled | lleno |

It's filled with flowers.

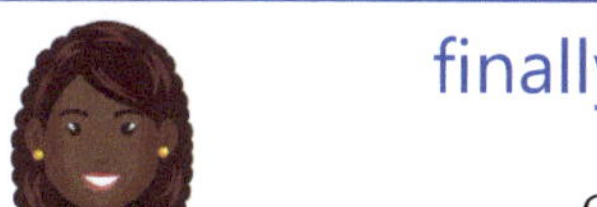

| finally | finalmente |

She finally smiled.

| fine | multa |

He had to pay a fine.

| fly | volar |

Did you fly there?

| force | fuerza |

We learned about force.

| front | frente |

She was at the front of the line.

| full | completo |

The basket was full.

| game | juego |

Who won the game?

| gave | dio |

He gave her flowers.

| government | gobierno |

We learned about the government.

| green | verde |

The frog is green.

| half | medio |

I hate half the orange.

| heat | calor |

Please heat up the oven.

| heavy | pesado |

It's really heavy.

| hot | caliente |

The coffee is hot.

| inches | pulgadas |

How many inches is it?

| include | incluir |

They made sure to include sunscreen.

| inside | dentro |

He was inside the dog house.

| island | isla |

The island was beautiful.

| known | conocido |

They've known each other forever.

| language | idioma |

Do you know sign language?

| less | Menos |

Three is less than five.

| machine | máquina |

It's grandma's sewing machine.

material — material

She needed material.

minutes — minutos

How many minutes left?

note — Nota

She left a note.

nothing — nada

He had nothing he had to do.

noun — sustantivo

Is that a noun or a verb?

object — objeto

We measured each object.

ocean — Oceano

I love the ocean.

oh — Oh

Oh! It's a puppy!

pair — par

Are those your pair of shoes?

person — persona

He's a smart person.

plane — avión

Is it your first time on a plane?

power — poder

What super power do you have?

produce — Produce

It will produce vegetables.

quickly — con rapidez

The greyhound ran quickly.

ran — corrió

They ran the race.

rest — relajarse

You needed to rest.

road — la carretera

Is this the right road?

round — redondo

The soccer ball is round.

rule — regla

Which rule did you break?

scientists — científico

They are scientists.

shape — forma

What shape is that?

shown — mostrado

The photo was shown to me.

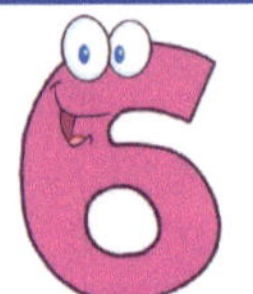

six — seis

He rolled a six.

size — Talla

What's your shoe size?

special — *especial*

It's a special cake.

stars — *estrellas*

How many stars did you earn?

stay — *permanecer*

She knows stay.

stood — *destacado*

He stood at the teacher's desk.

street — *calle*

It's on this street.

strong — *fuerte*

How strong are you?

surface — *superficie*

Most of the Earth's surface is water.

system — *sistema*

Tell me about the solar system.

ten — *diez*

Did you hit all ten pins?

though — *aunque*

Even though she's busy, she read alot.

thousands — *miles*

Thousands of people live here.

understand — *entender*

Do you understand the homework?

verb — *verbo*

Which word is a verb?

wait — *Espere*

How long did you wait?

warm — *calentar*

How warm is the soup?

week — *semana*

This week is busy.

wheels — *ruedas*

Did you buy new wheels?

yes — *si*

Yes, I want to go.

yet — *todavía*

Are we there yet?

anything — *cualquier cosa*

Do cows eat anything but grass?

arms — *brazo*

She crossed her arms.

beautiful — *hermoso*

The area is beautiful.

believe — *creer*

I believe in Santa Claus.

beside — *junto a*

They stood beside one another.

bill — cuenta

Did you receive the bill?

blue — azul

It's a blue butterfly.

brother — hermano

Is that your brother?

can't — no puedo

When I can't sleep, I count sheep.

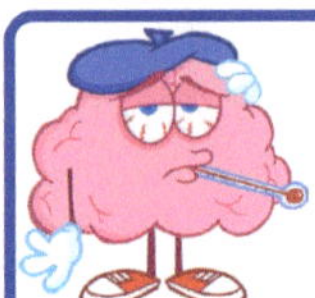

cause — porque

What's the cause?

cells — células

We learned about cells.

center — centrar

The bullseye is the center.

clothes — ropa

Did you hang your clothes up?

dance — baile

They dance like professionals.

describe — describir

Describe the colors.

developed — desarrollar

They developed a strong friendship.

difference — diferencia

What's the difference?

direction — dirección

Which direction do we go?

discovered — descubrir

Who discovered antibiotics?

distance — distancia

What's the distance to there?

divided — dividir

It was divided up.

drive — conducir

Does your dad drive you?

drop — soltar

Did you drop and crack it?

edge — borde

I stood at the edge of the pond.

eggs — huevos

Do you have enough eggs?

energy — energía

Have you used solar energy?

Europe — Europa

Are you going to visit Europe?

exercise — ejercicio

We all should exercise.

farmers — agricultores

Farmers work hard.

felt — sensación

He felt happy with friends.

finished — terminar

He finished his painting.

flowers — flores

Flowers are growing there.

forest — bosque

Where is the forest?

general — general

We shopped at the general store.

gone — ido

Has he gone fishing?

grass — césped

Will you cut the grass?

happy — contento

Music made him happy.

heart — corazón

Did you draw a heart?

held — retenida

They held hands.

instruments — instrumentos

What instruments do you play?

interest — interesar

I have an interest in flowers.

job — trabajo

What job did you chose?

kept — mantener

She kept hold of the balloon.

lay — laico

Will she lay an egg?

legs — piernas

A cricket has six legs.

length — longitud

What's the length?

love — amor

Families love each other.

main — principal

There's the main gate.

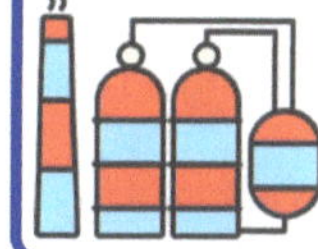

matter — importar

What are the states of matter?

meet — reunirse

Do you want to meet them?

members — miembros

All the members were there.

million — millón

She watched a million how-to videos.

mind — mente

Your mind is full of imagination.

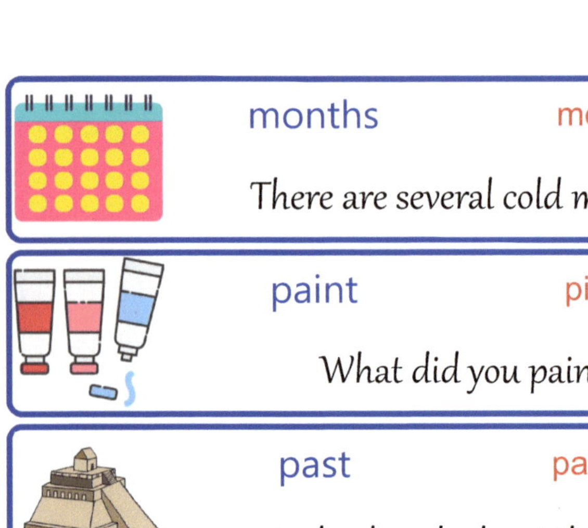

months — *meses*

There are several cold months.

moon — *Luna*

The wolf howled at the moon.

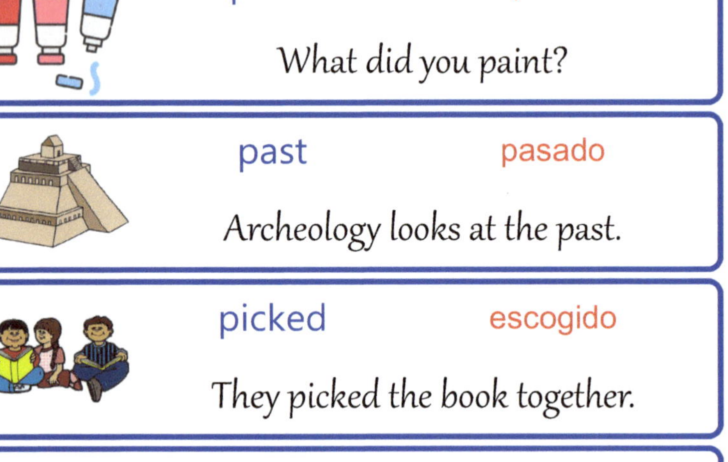

paint — *pintar*

What did you paint?

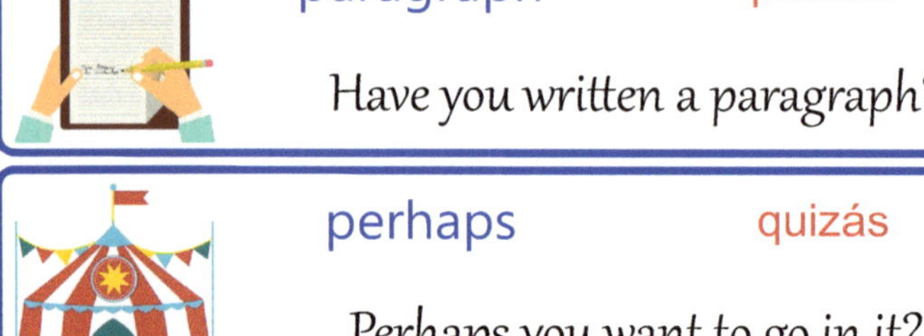

paragraph — *párrafo*

Have you written a paragraph?

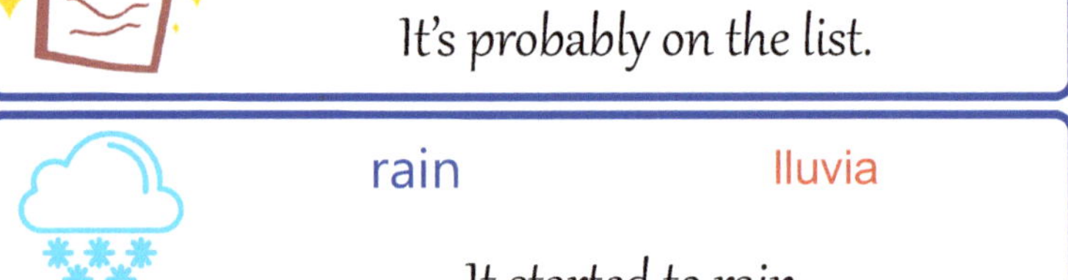

past — *pasado*

Archeology looks at the past.

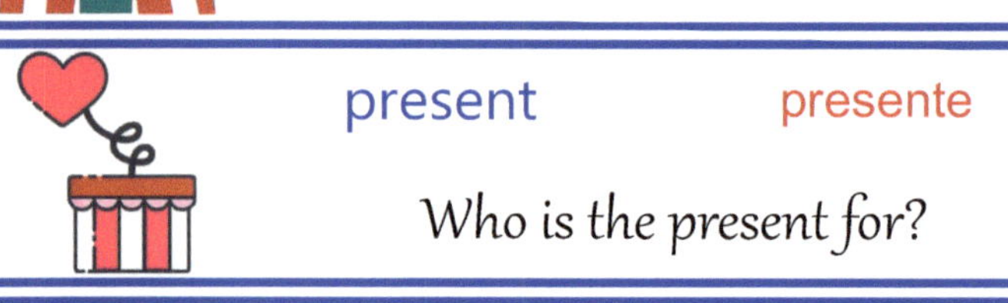

perhaps — *quizás*

Perhaps you want to go in it?

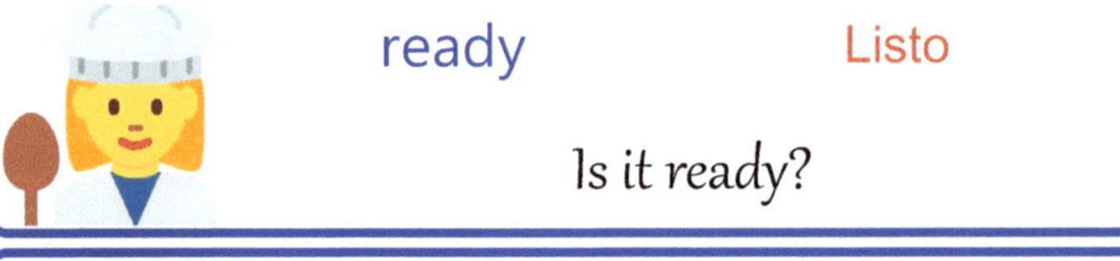

picked — *escogido*

They picked the book together.

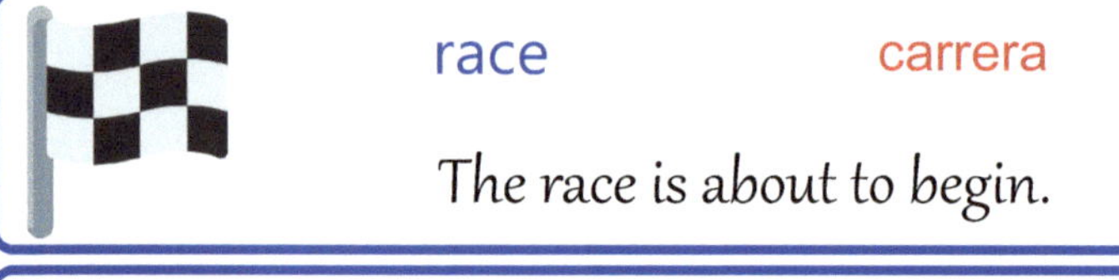

present — *presente*

Who is the present for?

probably — *probablemente*

It's probably on the list.

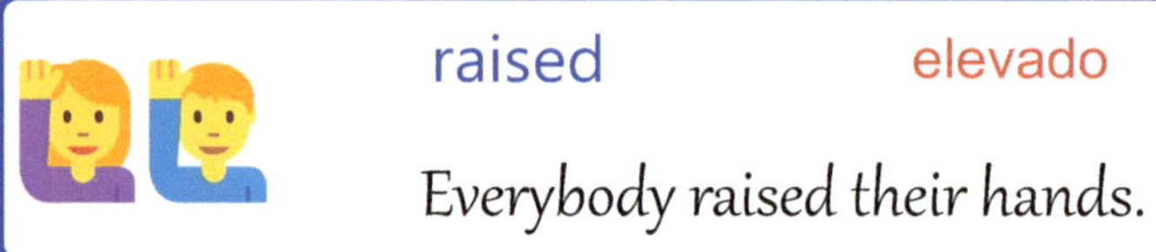

race — *carrera*

The race is about to begin.

rain — *lluvia*

It started to rain.

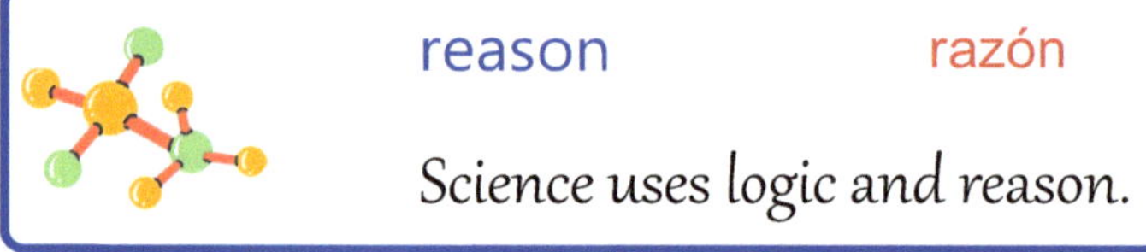

raised — *elevado*

Everybody raised their hands.

ready — *Listo*

Is it ready?

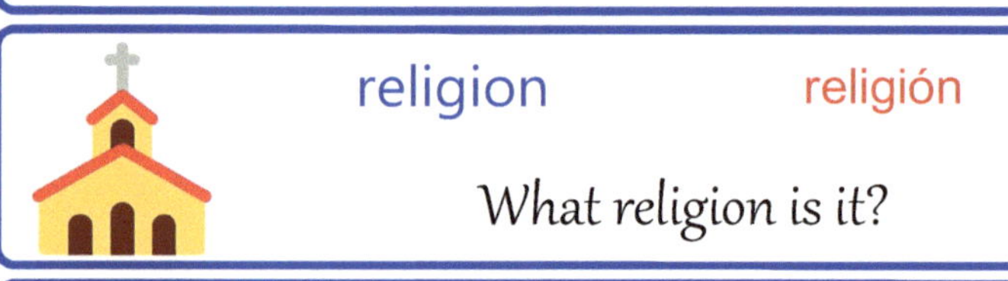

reason — *razón*

Science uses logic and reason.

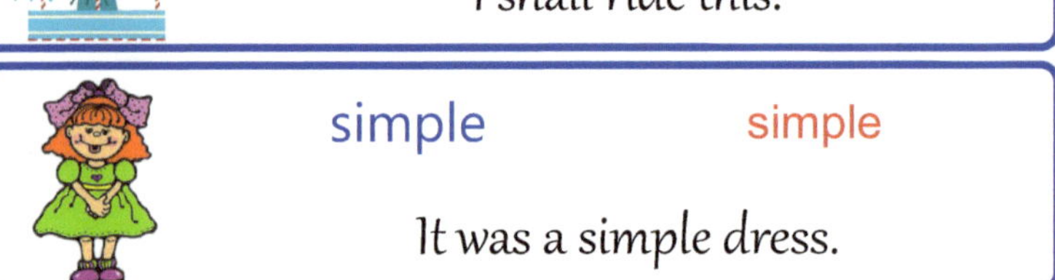

record — *grabar*

Who broke the record?

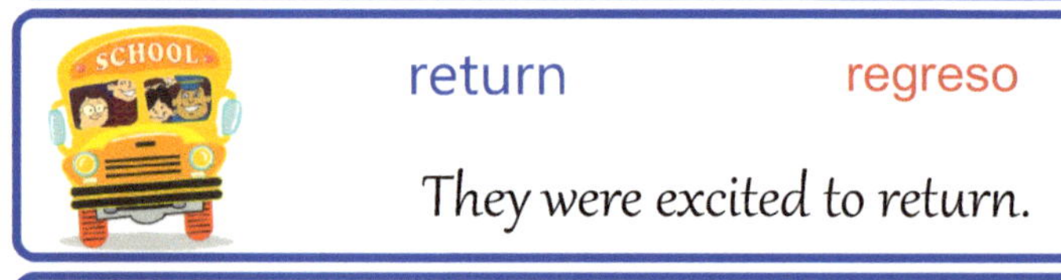

religion — *religión*

What religion is it?

represent — *representar*

He drew pictures to represent words.

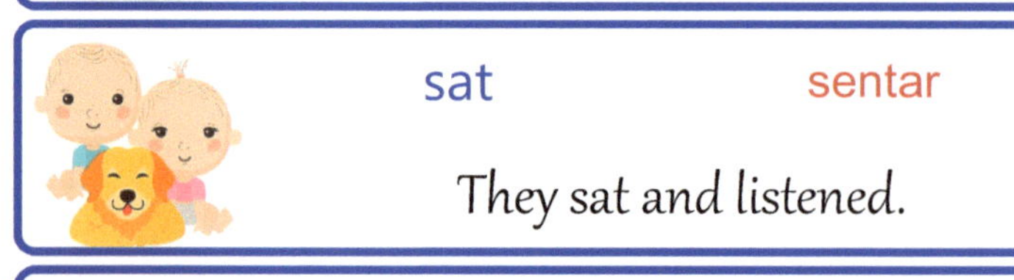

return — *regreso*

They were excited to return.

root — *raíz*

Which team do you root for?

sat — *sentar*

They sat and listened.

shall — *deberá*

I shall ride this.

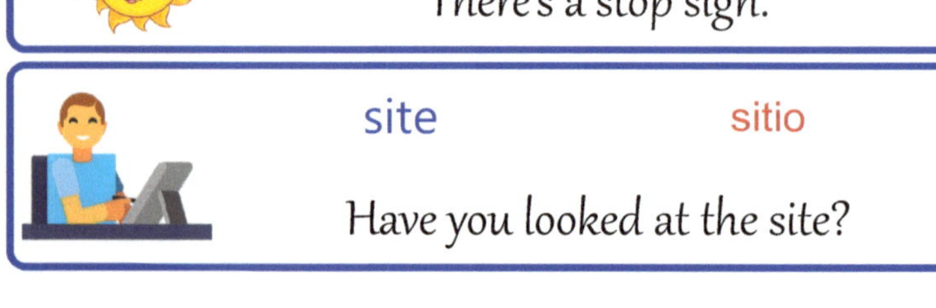

sign — *firmar*

There's a stop sign.

simple — *simple*

It was a simple dress.

site — *sitio*

Have you looked at the site?

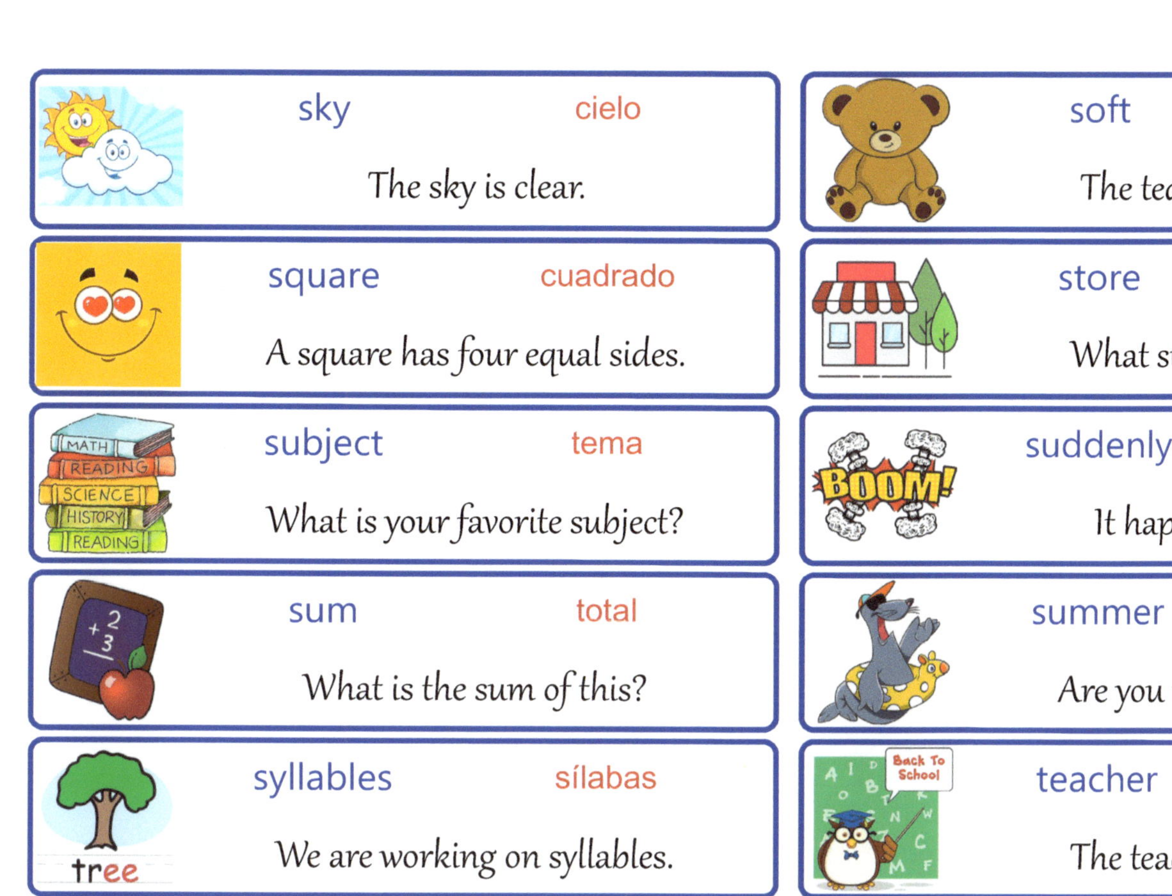

sky	cielo	The sky is clear.
soft	suave	The teddy bear is so soft.
square	cuadrado	A square has four equal sides.
store	Tienda	What store did you go to?
subject	tema	What is your favorite subject?
suddenly	repentinamente	It happened suddenly.
sum	total	What is the sum of this?
summer	verano	Are you ready for summer?
syllables	sílabas	We are working on syllables.
teacher	profesor	The teacher read to them.
test	prueba	How'd you do on the test?
third	tercero	How did you like third grade?
train	entrenar	We have a Christmas train.
wall	pared	She painted the wall.
weather	clima	What is the weather like?
west	Oeste	You need to go west.

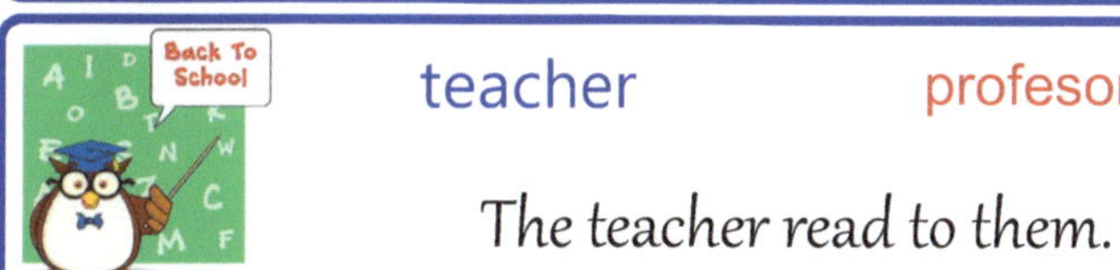

whether — ya sea — Whether you go by bus or not, go.

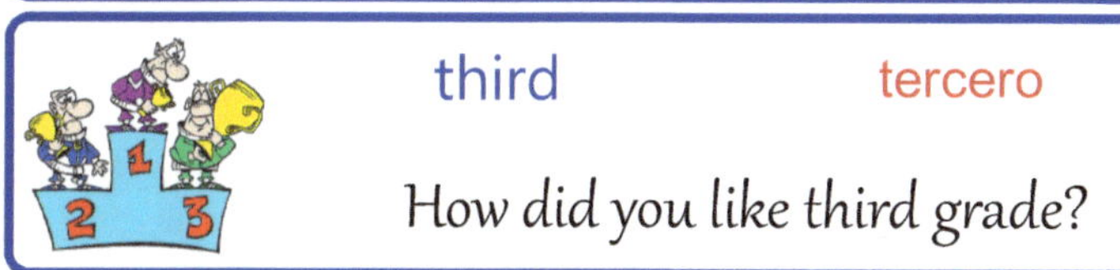

wide — amplio — How wide is the box?

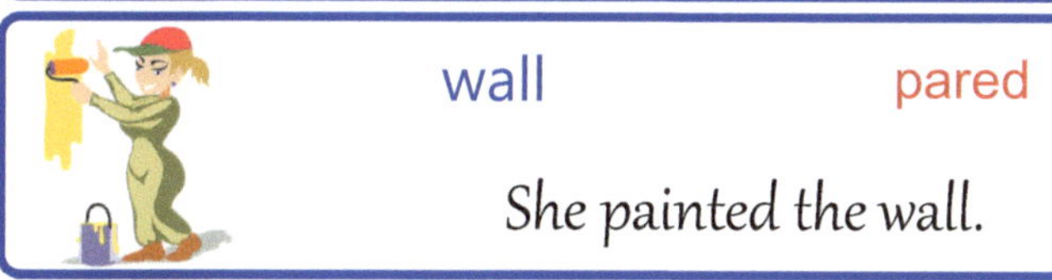

wild — salvaje — What is your favorite wild animal?

window — ventanas — Plants are in the window.

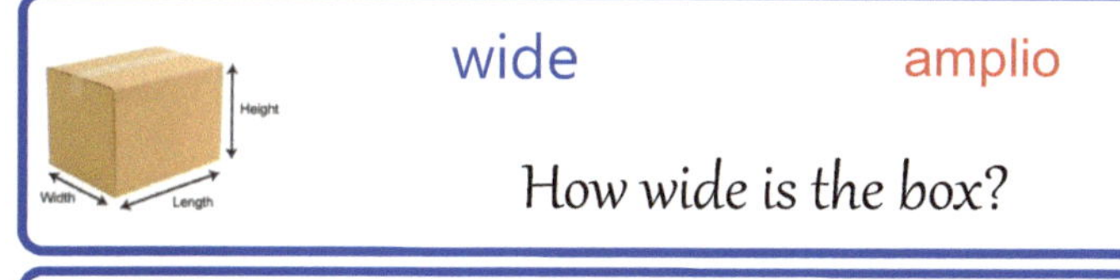

winter — invierno — Winter is here!

wish — deseo — Make a wish!

written — escrito — It was written down.

act — Actuar — Do you like to act in a play?

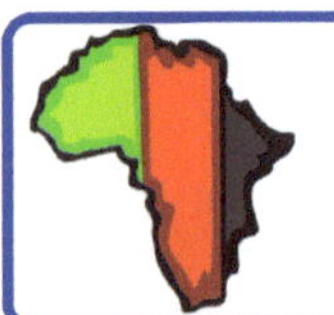
Africa — África
Did you vist Southern Africa?

age — años
They were around the same age

already — ya
I already bought groceries.

although — a pesar de que
Although sunny, it's cold out.

amount — cantidad
What amount of work do you have left?

angle — ángulo
Please measure the angle.

appear — Aparecer
You appear to be lost.

baby — bebé
Is this your baby?

bear — oso
He loves his old teddy bear.

beat — golpear
Our team beat yours.

bed — cama
We have a bunk bed.

bottom — fondo
There's treasure at the bottom.

bright — brillante
The sun is really bright.

broken — roto
Her heart is broken.

build — construir
What are you going to build?

buy — comprar
Did you buy a new car?

care — cuidado
She'll care for him.

case — caso
Don't forget your case.

cat — gato
I adopted a cat.

century — siglo
They said it's a century old.

consonant — consonante
What is the consonant?

copy — Copiar
Is the copy machine working?

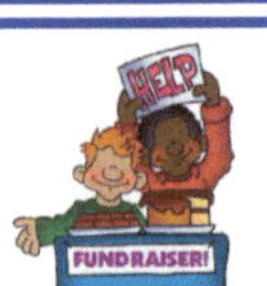
couldn't — no puedo
Couldn't we throw a fundraiser?

count — contar
How high can you count?

cross — cruzar

There's a cross on the church.

dictionary — diccionario

You may use a dictionary.

died — murió

I didn't charge my phone and it died.

dress — vestir

She loved her new dress.

either — ya sea

Will either of you wash the car?

everyone — todos

Everyone was working.

everything — todo

Everything here is fun.

exactly — exactamente

It was exactly as she imagined.

factors — factores

What are the factors of these numbers?

flight — vuelo

The helicopter took flight.

fingers — dedos

Cross your fingers.

floor — suelo

Did you mop the floor?

fraction — fracción

What fraction of the cake did you eat?

free — gratis

They set the tiger free.

French — francés

She's a French bull dog.

gold — oro

She had a gold star.

hair — cabello

Did you get get your hair cut?

hill — colina

The sun peaked over the hill.

hole — agujero

Did you get a hole-in-one?

hope — esperanza

Let's hope.

ice — hielo

The ice was melting.

instead — en lugar

Do you drink tea instead of coffee?

iron — hierro

I need to iron my shirt.

jumped — saltar

The cow jumped over the moon.

 **killed** — *delicado*
Pest control killed the bugs.

 **lake** — *lago*
We're still going to the lake.

 **laughed** — *Se rió*
They all laughed.

 **lead** — *líder*
We were in the lead.

 **let's** — *vamos*
Let's go to the fair!

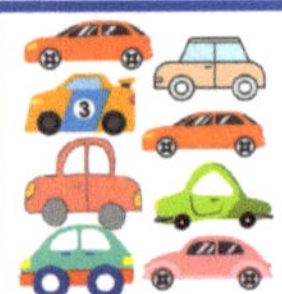 **lot** — *lote*
The car lot was full.

 **melody** — *melodía*
What a beautiful melody.

 **metal** — *metal*
They have a metal trashcan.

 **method** — *método*
We use the scientific method.

 **middle** — *medio*
She stood in the middle.

 **milk** — *Leche*
Did you drink your milk?

 **moment** — *momento*
Wait a moment for the bus.

 **nation** — *nación*
Which nation are you from?

 **natural** — *natural*
This place has natural beauty.

 **outside** — *fuera de*
They brought sand in from outside.

 **per** — *por*
It's forty dollars per car.

 **phrase** — *frase*
His phrase inlcuded a penny.

 **poor** — *pobre*
Did you do poor on the exam?

 **possible** — *posible*
Will it be possible to grill this weekend?

 **pounds** — *libras*
The price was in pounds.

 **pushed** — *empujado*
She pushed the stroller.

 **quiet** — *tranquilo*
Quiet in the library.

 **quite** — *bastante*
You are quite busy

 **remain** — *permanecer*
Please remain in your seat.

 **result** — resultado
What was the result of the election?

 **ride** — paseo
Let's ride bikes!

 **rolled** — arrollado
The diploma was rolled up.

 **sail** — vela
Do you like to sail?

 **scale** — escala
Use the scale to weigh them.

 **section** — sección
This section is fenced off

 **sleep** — dormir
It's time to sleep.

 **smiled** — sonreí
He always smiled

 **snow** — nieve
Let's play in the snow!

 **soil** — suelo
Plant it in the soil.

 **solve** — resolver
Did you solve the equation?

 **someone** — alguien
Someone cleaned their desk.

 **son** — hijo
Is that your son?

 **speak** — hablar
Who will speak next?

 **speed** — velocidad
What's the speed limit?

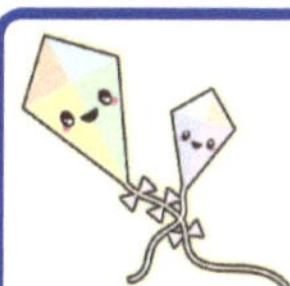 **spring** — primavera
Is it finally spring?

 **stone** — Roca
She skipped a stone across the pond.

 **surprise** — sorpresa
She threw a surprise party.

 **tall** — alto
How tall is a giraffe?

 **temperature** — temperatura
What's the temperature?

 **themselves** — sí mismos
They enjoyed themselves.

 **tiny** — minúsculo
It's so tiny.

 **trip** — viaje
Did you enjoy your road trip?

 **type** — tipo
What type of project is it?

 village — pueblo

We travled to the village.

 within — dentro

What did you see within the museum.

 wonder — preguntarse

I wonder what we'll see!

 alone — solo

While alone, he read.

 art — Arte

Do you like to look at art?

 bad — malo

The movie was bad.

 bank — banco

I need to go to the bank.

 bit — poco

I bit the apple.

 break — rotura

Time for a break.

 brown — marrón

It's a brown cow.

 burning — ardiente

The candles were burning.

 business — negocio

They opened their business.

 captain — capitán

Who is the ship's captain?

 catch — captura

Did you catch the ball?

 caught — atrapado

You caught a fish.

 cents — centavos

That's just my two cents.

 child — niño

The child prayed.

 choose — escoger

Which one did you choose?

 clean — limpiar

Did you clean?

 climbed — subido

They climbed it.

 cloud — nube

We watched the storm cloud.

 coast — costa

The coast is relaxing.

 continued — continuado

He continued to look through the box.

 control — controlar

Who has the remote control?

 **cool** — *frio*
That's a cool car.

 **cost** — *costo*
They cut the cost.

 **decimal** — *decimal*
Where does the decimal go?

 **desert** — *Desierto*
Have you been to the desert?

 **design** — *diseño*
Did you design this?

 **direct** — *directo*
Did you direct the film?

 **drawing** — *dibujo*
Is that your drawing?

 **ears** — *orejas*
Did you get your ears pierced?

 **east** — *este*
Are you from the east coast?

 **else** — *más*
Did you draw that or did someone else?

 **engine** — *motor*
The fire engine parked there.

 **England** — *Inglaterra*
I want to go to England.

 **equal** — *igual*
Does it equal four?

 **experiment** — *experimentar*
What was your experiment?

 **express** — *Rápido*
They have express delivery.

 **feeling** — *sensación*
He's feeling sick.

 **fell** — *cayó*
I fell down the stairs.

 **flow** — *fluir*
We created a flow chart.

 **foot** — *pie*
Twelve inches is a foot.

 **garden** — *jardín*
She worked in the garden

 **gas** — *gas*
We stopped to get gas.

 **glass** — *vaso*
Did you clean the glass?

 **God** — *Dios*
Many believe in God and angels.

 **grew** — *creció*
The flower grew.

 **history** — historia

She taught history.

 **human** — humano

We learned about the human body.

 **hunting** — caza

We're hunting for Easting eggs.

 **increase** — incrementar

Did the house value increase?

 **information** — información

He took in so much information.

 **itself** — sí mismo

The house won't clean itself.

 **joined** — unido

I joined them at the cafe.

 **key** — llave

Did you find your key?

 **lady** — dama

The lady worked long hours.

 **law** — ley

It's the law.

 **least** — menos

Did you at least remember your bag?

 **lost** — perdió

Have you lost something?

 **maybe** — tal vez

Maybe we'll go rafting.

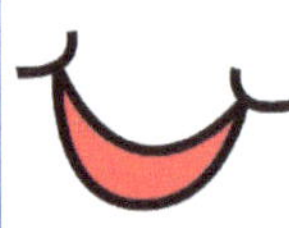 **mouth** — boca

Do your braces make your mouth hurt?

 **party** — fiesta

How was the party?

 **pay** — pagar

We need to pay

 **period** — período

You put a period at the end.

 **plains** — llanuras

The road went through the plains

 **please** — Por favor

Please have breakfast.

 **practice** — práctica

They were at practice.

 **president** — presidente

Make sure you vote for president

 **received** — recibido

She received an award.

 **report** — reporte

Your report card looks great!

 **ring** — anillo

Such a beautiful ring!

rise — subir

We were waiting for the sun to rise.

save — salvar

Try to save some money.

sent — expedido

Was the email sent?

serve — servir

Did you serve that table?

single — soltero

A single balloon

statement — declaración

He worked on his thesis statement.

straight — Derecho

It's a straight road.

student — estudiante

The students worked together

symbols — símbolos

What do those symbols mean?

touch — toque

The cheerleader can touch her toes

uncle — tío

We learned about Uncle Sam.

visit — visitar

They went to visit their grandparents.

row — fila

Did you go out on row boats?

seeds — semillas

Did you get seeds for the garden?

separate — separar

The brain has separate parts.

shouted — gritó

The cheerleaders shouted their cheer.

skin — piel

She used a mask for her skin.

stick — palo

It's your hockey stick.

strange — extraño

That's strange looking.

suppose — suponer

I suppose we could go to the pool.

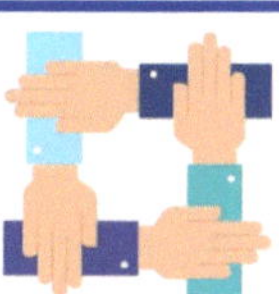

team — equipo

Are you on the basketball team?

trouble — problema

Did you have car trouble?

valley — Valle

They traveled to the valley.

wear — vestir

Did you find a suit to wear?

whose — *cuyo*

Whose guitar is it?

wire — *cable*

This telephone has a wire.

woman — *mujer*

Is the woman pregnant?

wrote — *escribió*

She wrote poetry

yard — *yarda*

Lucky is in the yard.

you're — *tú*

You're an angel.

yourself — *tú mismo*

Did you go hiking by yourself?

addition — *adición*

Do you learn addition?

army — *Ejército*

Is he joining the army?

bell — *campana*

Ring the bell.

belong — *pertenecer a*

They belong together.

block — *bloquear*

Did you have a toy block?

blood — *sangre*

I donated blood.

blow — *soplo*

Did you blow the bubbles?

board — *tablero*

That's her surf board

bones — *huesos*

Did you see the dinosaur bones?

branches — *ramas*

There are three branches.

cattle — *vacas*

We raise cattle.

chief — *jefe*

Is your dad the fire chief?

compare — *comparar*

You can't compare apples to oranges.

compound — *compuesto*

This is a compound.

consider — *considerar*

Did you consider it?

cook — *cocinar*

What did you cook?

corner — *esquina*

Turn at that corner.

crops — cultivos

How are the crops growing?

crowd — multitud

There was a large crowd.

current — Actual

Are these your current goals?

doctor — médico

He went to see the doctor.

dollars — dolares

How many hundreds of dollars is it?

eight — ocho

Did you hit the eight ball?

electric — eléctrico

Do you own an electric car?

elements — elementos

Look at the periodic table of elements.

enjoy — disfrutar

Did you enjoy your coffee?

entered — ingresó

She entered the room.

except — excepto

like all vegetables except peas.

exciting — emocionante

This is so exciting!

expect — esperar

When do you expect the baby?

famous — famoso

She's a famous actress.

fit — ajuste

How much did you fit in there?

flat — plano

The tire was flat.

fruit — Fruta

Watermelon is my favorite fruit.

fun — divertido

They had fun at the beach

guess — adivinar

Guess how many

hat — sombrero

I like your new hat.

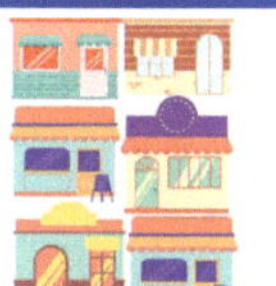

hit — golpear

They hit up a lot of stores.

indicate — indicar

Did you indicate that you are ill?

industry — industria

This is where the industry is.

insects — insectos

Do you like insects?

interesting — *interesante*
The dog thought the toy was interesting.

lie — *mentira*
It's never good to lie.

loud — *ruidoso*
The concert is loud.

mall — *centro comercial*
Do you want to go to the mall?

mine — *mía*
Be mine.

movement — *movimiento*
Movement is important.

observe — *observar*
Do you want to observe the stars?

particular — *especial*
I prefer a particular ketchup.

poem — *poema*
Would you read your poem?

position — *posición*
She likes sitting in that position.

property — *propiedad*
That property is for sale.

rather — *más bien*
I'd rather be reading.

Japanese — *japonés*
These are Japanese cherry blossoms.

lifted — *levantado*
The jeep is lifted.

major — *mayor*
What's your college major?

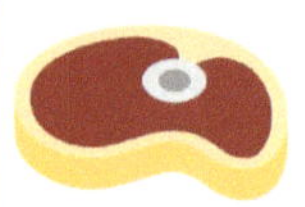
meat — *carne*
Do you eat meat?

modern — *moderno*
She loves modern art.

necessary — *necesario*
It is necessary to go to school.

park — *parque*
Let's go to the park.

planets — *planetas*
We were learning about the planets.

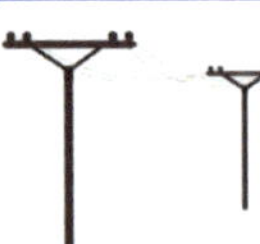
pole — *polo*
Is that a telephone pole?

process — *proceso*
Is that the process?

provide — *proporcionar*
We wanted to provide food.

rhythm — *ritmo*
That's your heart's rhythm.

rich	Rico	I want to be rich.
safe	seguro	Do you have a safe?
sand	arena	They played in the sand.
science	Ciencias	We love science.
sell	vender	She is going to sell lemonade.
send	enviar	Did you send the letter?
sense	sentido	What sense did you just use?
seven	Siete	She has seven lipsticks.
sharp	agudo	Those are sharp scissors.
shoulder	hombro	Did you hurt your shoulder?
 sigh	suspiro	Did you sigh?
silent	silencio	Please be silent in the library.
soldiers	soldados	They are soldiers.
spot	Mancha	It's a red spot.
spread	propagar	Spread your wings.
stream	corriente	We played at the stream.
string	cuerda	It's a red string.
suggested	sugirió	I suggested you do your homework.
supply	suministro	Did you supply what you needed?
swim	nadar	Let's go for a swim!
terms	condiciones	Did you learn new vocabulary terms?
thick	grueso	That's a thick book.
thin	Delgado	That's a thin book.
thus	así	I was tired, thus I didn't go to the party.

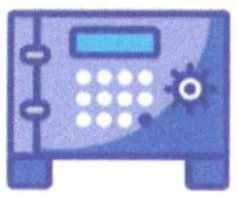

tied — atado

Did you tie a knot?

tone — tono

He said he's tone deaf.

trade — comercio

I'll trade you my sandwich for yours.

tube — tubo

That's my tube of toothpaste.

value — valor

The value of family is greater.

wash — lavar

We decided to wash the car.

wasn't — no era

Wasn't that your cousin?

weight — peso

The scale will measure your weight.

wife — esposa

His wife is a teacher.

wings — alas

She was flapping her wings.

won't — no lo hará

Won't you go fishing with me?

a — uno

A girl sang.

about — acerca de

It's about lunch time.

all — todas

It's all gone!

an — uno

I have an idea!

and — y

I like cats and dogs.

are — son

We are friends.

as — como

It's light as a feather.

at — a

You're at school.

be — ser

We'll be reading.

been — estado

I've been to Mexico.

but — pero

I like peas, but not cabbage.

by — por

John sat by Jane.

called — llamado

I need to call my mom

can — lata
Can you go to the zoo?

come — ven
Will you come to the park?

could — podría
Could you see the moon?

day — día
What day is it today?

Days of the Week
Sunday
Monday
Tuesday
Wednesday
Thursday
Friday
Saturday

did — hizo
Did you buy popcorn?

do — hacer
Do you like pizza?

down — abajo
We walked down the stairs.

each — cada
They were one dollar each.

find — encontrar
Did you find your keys?

first — primera
He earned first place.

for — para
We ate turkey for Thanksgiving.

from — desde
I am from Texas.

TEXAS

get — obtener
Did you get your report card?

go — Vamos
May we go to recess?

had — tenía
Mrs. Smith had a cold.

has — tiene
Lily has a cat.

have — tener
Do you have a pencil?

he — él
he waved hello.

her — su
It is her doll.

him — él
John sat next to him.

his — su
It's his soccer ball.

how — cómo
How was the football game?

I — yo
I like icecream.

if — Si
If you are sick, go see the nurse.

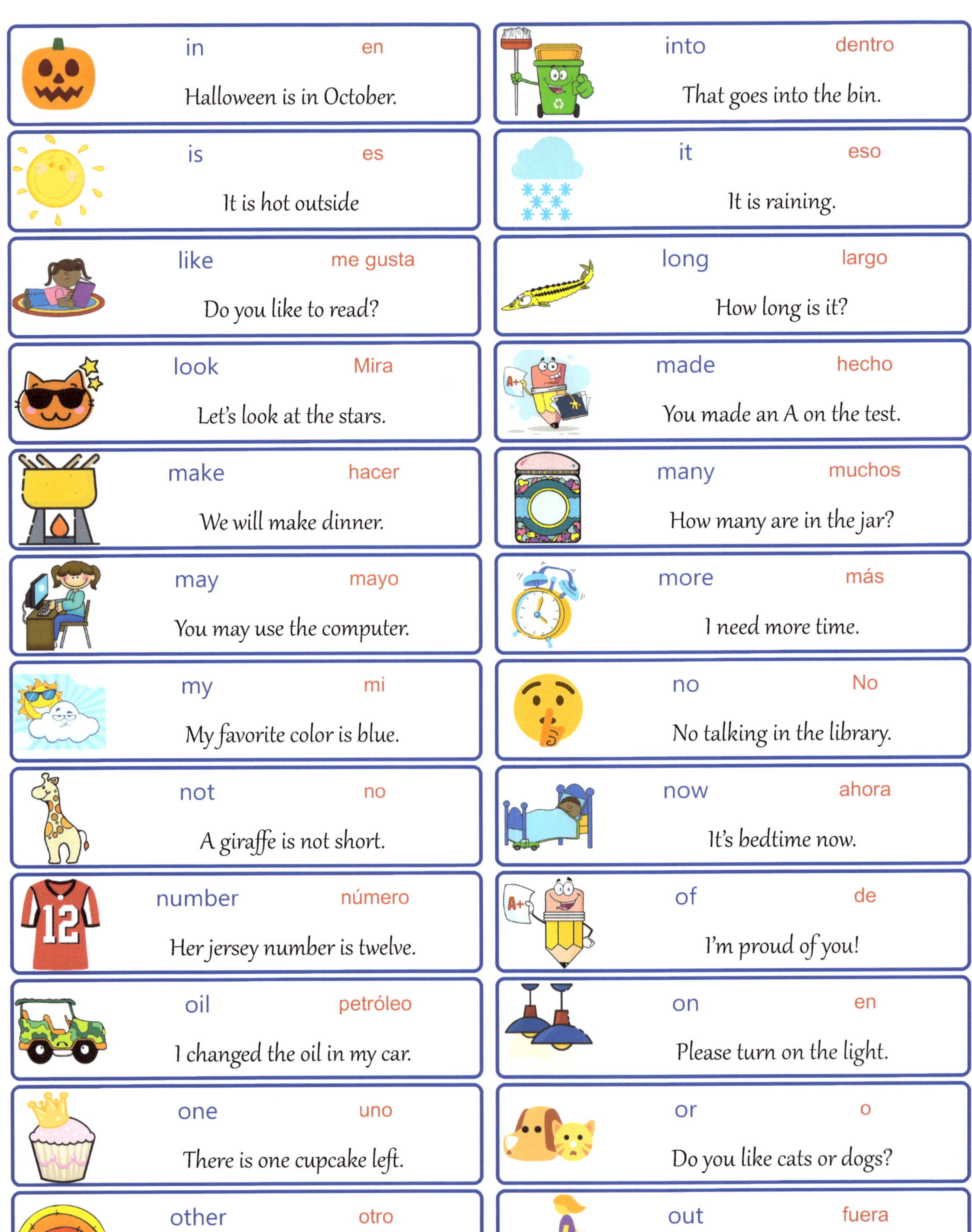

in — en
Halloween is in October.

into — dentro
That goes into the bin.

is — es
It is hot outside

it — eso
It is raining.

like — me gusta
Do you like to read?

long — largo
How long is it?

look — Mira
Let's look at the stars.

made — hecho
You made an A on the test.

make — hacer
We will make dinner.

many — muchos
How many are in the jar?

may — mayo
You may use the computer.

more — más
I need more time.

my — mi
My favorite color is blue.

no — No
No talking in the library.

not — no
A giraffe is not short.

now — ahora
It's bedtime now.

number — número
Her jersey number is twelve.

of — de
I'm proud of you!

oil — petróleo
I changed the oil in my car.

on — en
Please turn on the light.

one — uno
There is one cupcake left.

or — o
Do you like cats or dogs?

other — otro
What other colors do we need?

out — fuera
Take the dog out for a walk.

part — parte
He ate part of my homework.

people — personas
A lot of people were dancing.

said — dijo
She said hello.

see — ver
He can't see without glasses.

she — ella
She had fun with her friends.

sit — sentar
She decided to sit.

so — entonces
We had so much fun.

some — algunos
I need some paper.

than — que
He is taller than her.

that — ese
That is my house.

the — uno
The weather is nice.

their — su
They liked their teacher.

them — ellos
I invited them to my party.

then — entonces
Do your chores, then you can play.

there — allí
It's over there.

these — estas
These are my markers.

they — ellos
They were jump roping.

this — esta
This is your backpack.

time — hora
What time is it?

to — a
I went to school.

two — dos
There are two owls.

up — arriba
We walked up the stairs.

use — utilizar
Let's use the pool.

was — fue
She was reading.

water	agua	Drink more water.
way	camino	It's a one way street.
we	nosotros	We went to the beach.
were	fueron	We were at the carnival.
what	qué	What is your question?
when	cuando	When is the dance?
which	cuales	Which snack do you want?
who	quién	Who likes hockey?
will	será	I will go to the park.
with	con	He had toast with his cereal.
words	palabras	You make words to play.
would	será	Would you like some juice?
write	escribir	Please write your name.
you	tú	You are strong.
your	tu	Your ball is here.

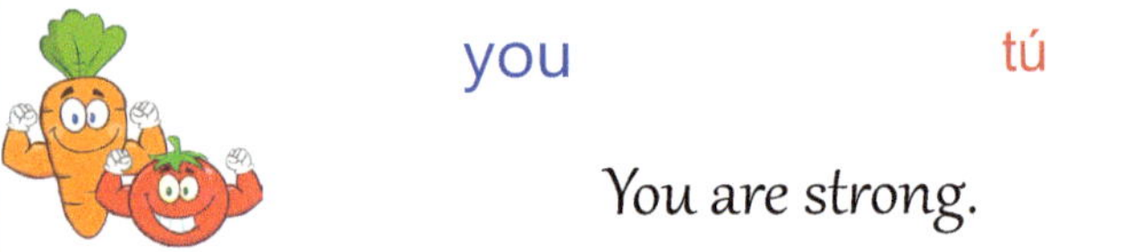